This coloring book belongs to :

____

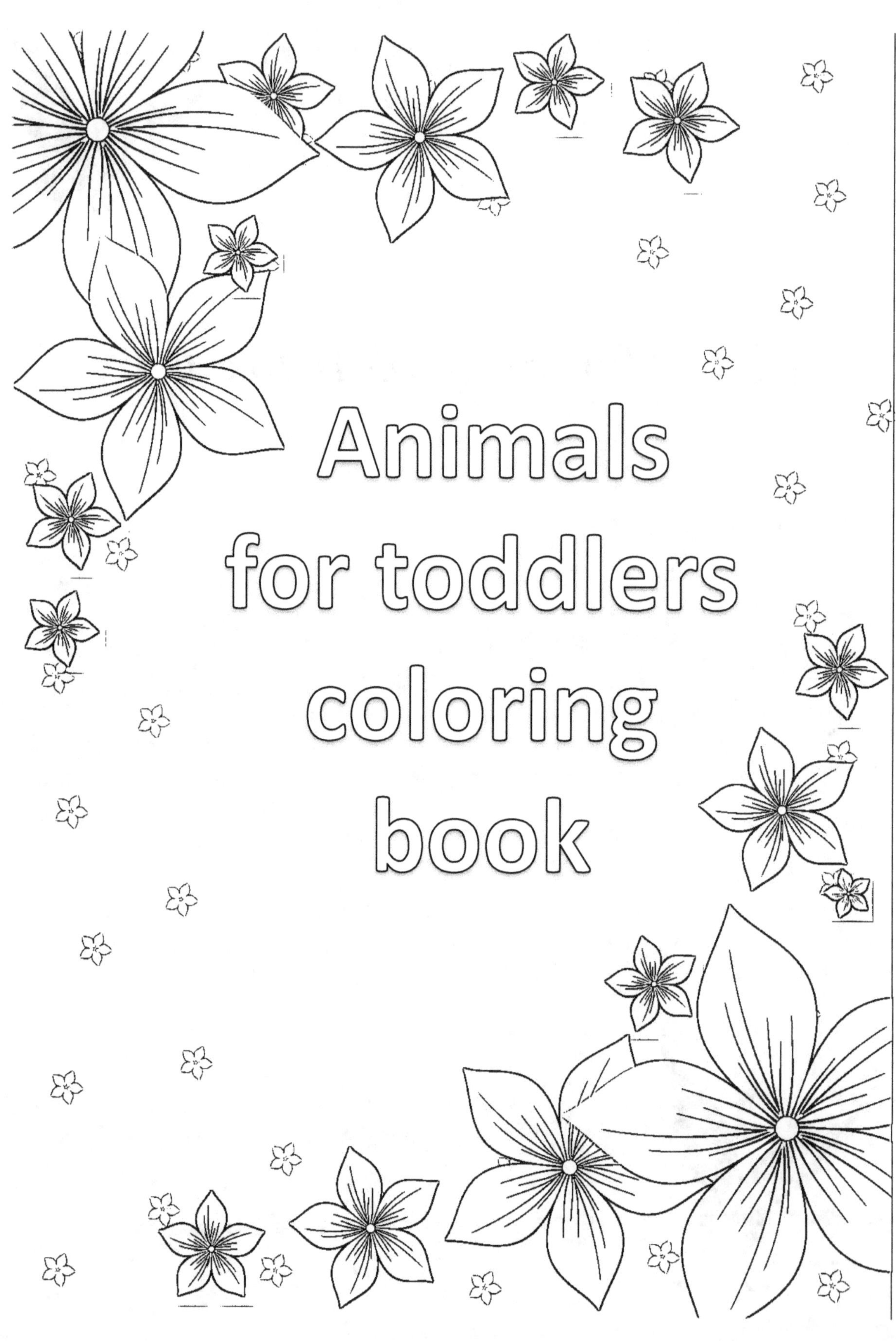

Animals for toddlers coloring book

Bear

Reindeer

Butterfly

Mouse

Cock

Turtle

Pig

Eagle

Ant

Camel

Giraffe

Ladybug

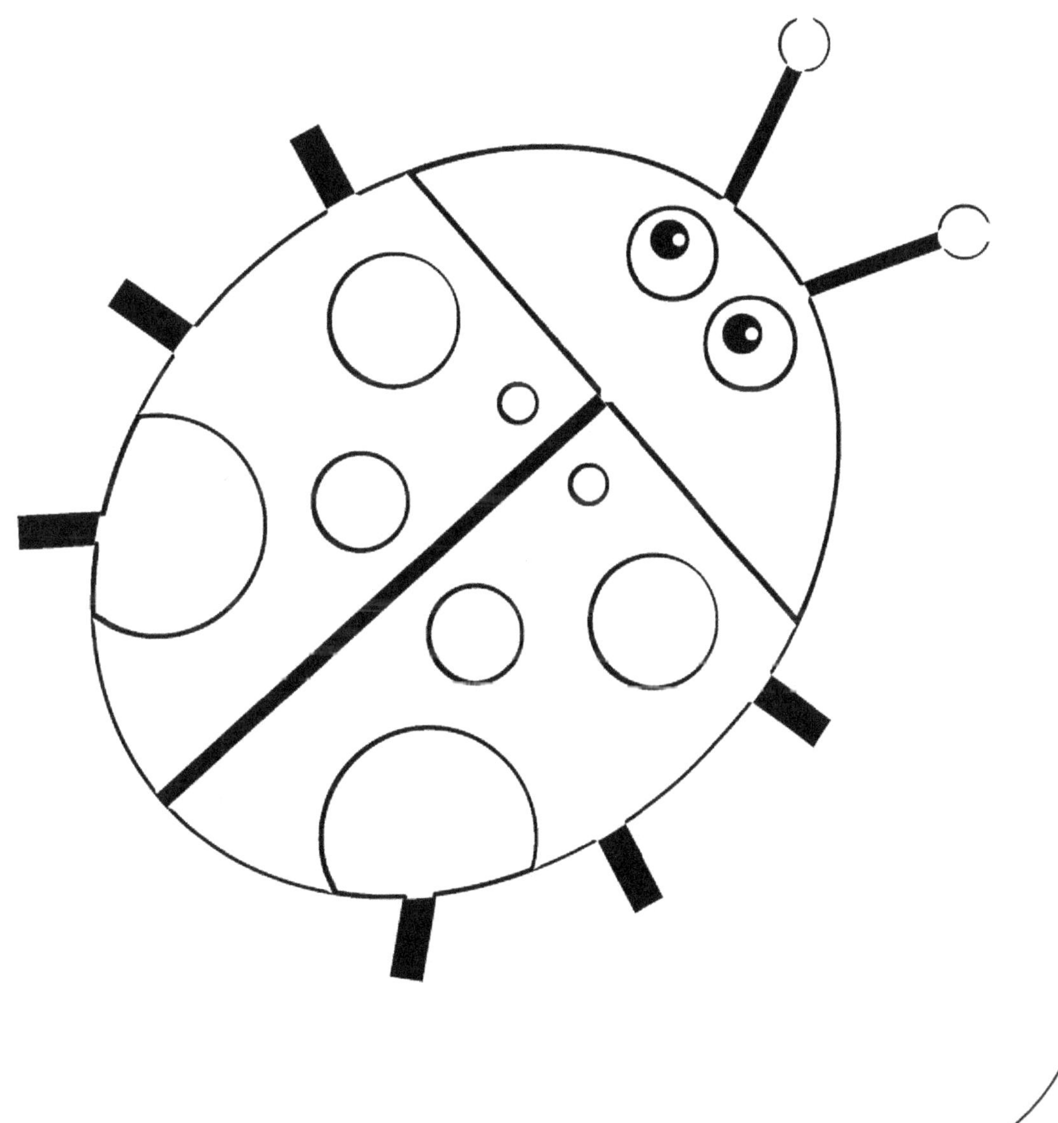

Squirrel

Bee

Sheep

Dog

Lion

Octopus

Parrot

Seahorse

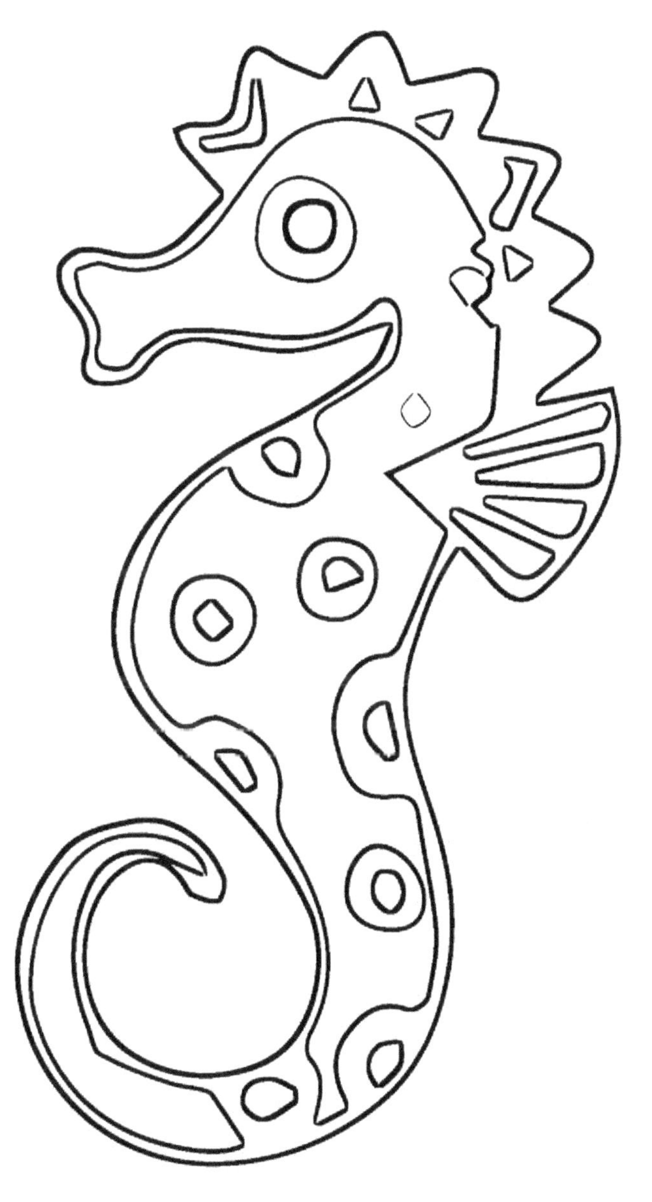

Fox

Duck

Rhino

Shark

Snake

Monkey

Deer

Fish

Owl

Frog

HEN

Whale

Tiger

Buffalo

Kangaroo

Peacock

Wolf

Goldfish

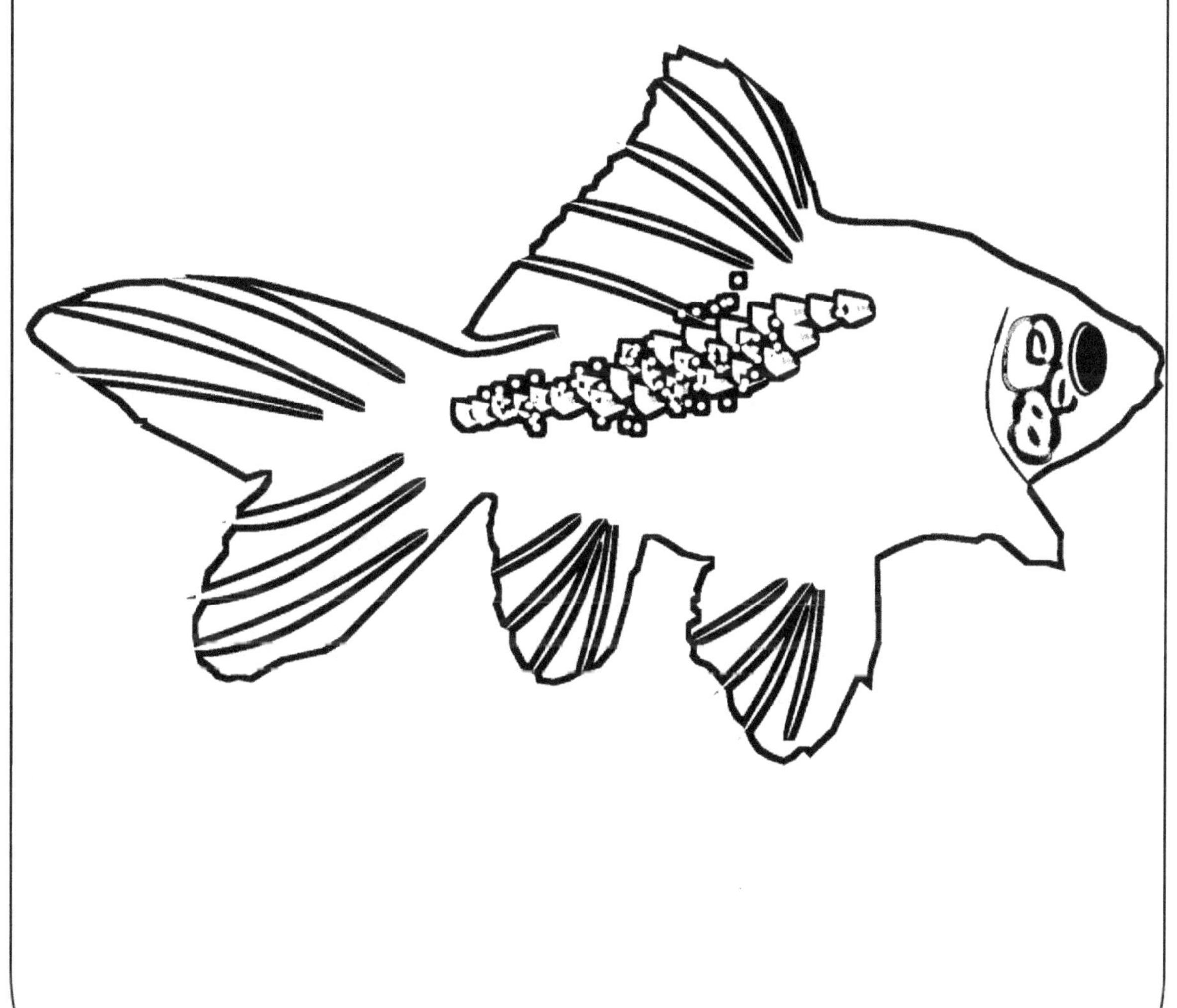

Turkey

Dolphin

Goat

Penguin

Unicorn

Hedgehog

Flamingo

Hummingbird

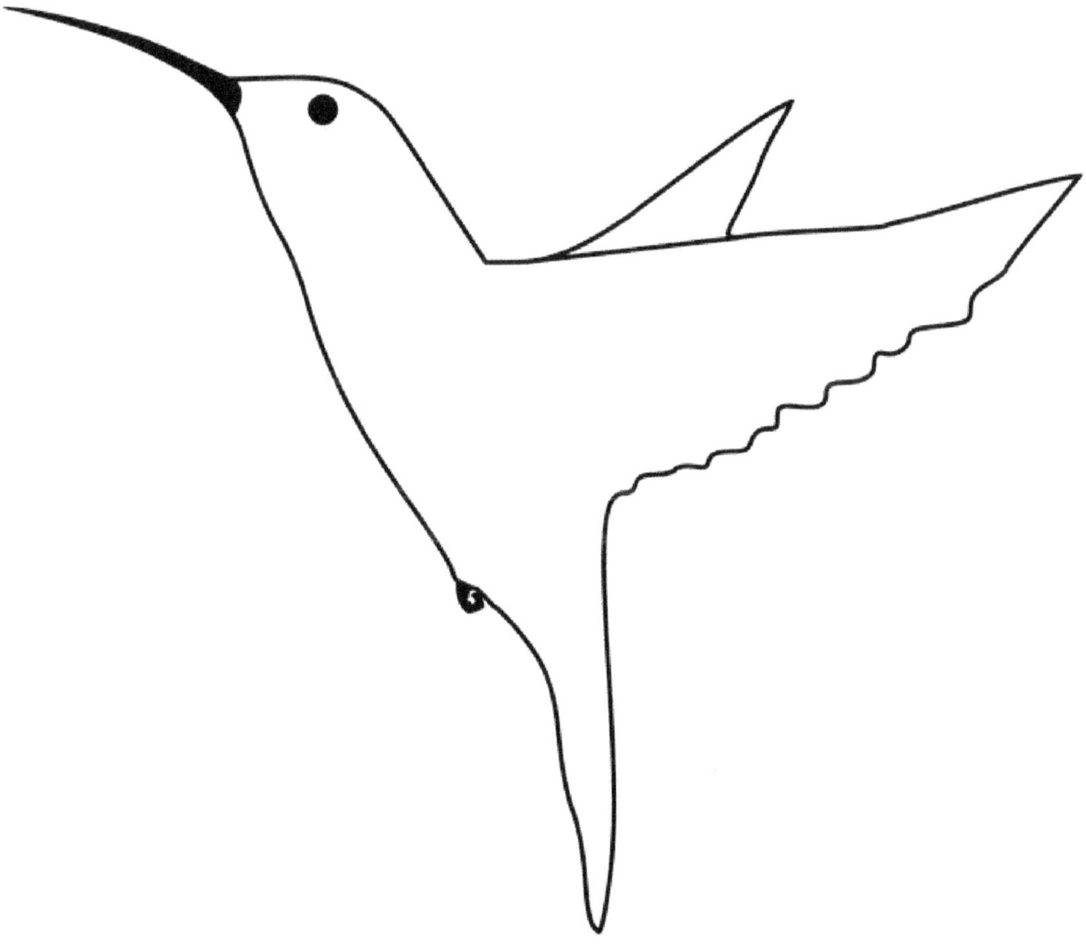

Spin

Horse

Cat

Cow

Donkey

Jellyfish

Panda bear

Koala

Bat

Hamster

Raccoon

Rabbit

Zebra

www.ingramcontent.com/pod-product-compliance
Lightning Source LLC
Chambersburg PA
CBHW081417250726

48654CB00013B/1730